Sofia love

our generation®

This is Sandy's story

SANDY™

OFF TO WINTER CAMP!

BY

SUSAN HUGHES

ILLUSTRATED BY GÉRALDINE CHARETTE

An Our Generation® *book*

MAISON BATTAT INC. *Publisher*

Characters portrayed in this book are fictitious. Any references to historical events, real people, or real locales are used fictitiously. Other names, characters, places, and incidents are products of the author's imagination, and any resemblance to actual events or locales or persons, living or dead, is entirely coincidental.

ISBN: 978-0-5786406-8-6
Printed in China

Read all the adventures in the
Our Generation® Book Series

1-One Smart Cookie
featuring Hally™

2-Blizzard on Moose Mountain
featuring Katelyn™

3-Stars in Your Eyes
featuring Sydney Lee™

4-The Note in the Piano
featuring Mary Lyn™

5-The Mystery of the Vanishing Coin
featuring Eva®

6-Adventures at Shelby Stables
featuring Lily Anna®

7-The Sweet Shoppe Mystery
featuring Jenny™

8-The Jumpstart Squad
featuring Juliet™

9-The Dress in the Window
featuring Audrey-Ann®

10-The Jukebox Babysitters
featuring Ashley-Rose®

11-In the Limelight
featuring Evelyn®

12-The Most Fantabulous Pajama Party Ever
featuring Willow™

13-Magic Under the Stars
featuring Shannon™

14-The Circus and the Secret Code
featuring Alice™

15-A Song from My Heart
featuring Layla™

16-Home Away from Home
featuring Ginger™

17-The Curious Castle
featuring Reese™

18-Stuck in the Middle of Knowhere
featuring Coral™

19-A Garden Where Friendship Grows
featuring Nahla™

20-A Fair Share at the Diner
featuring Isa™ & Noa™

21-The Incredible Ice Cream Project
featuring Lorelei™

22-Party Plans Go Pop!
featuring Sia™ & Sabina™

23-The Vacation of Hidden Charms
featuring Dedra™ & Denelle™

24-Finding a Home
featuring Naya™

25-A Love of Bowling
featuring Everly™

26-A Summer of Riding
featuring Tamera™ & Rashida™

27-The Foodie Friends Project
featuring Rayna™

28-Sneaky Santas
featuring Noelle™ & CJ™

29-The Jelly Bean Cinema
featuring Mienna™

30-All Aboard the OG Express
featuring Joanie™

31-Calling 9-1-1!
featuring Martha™ & Keisha™

32-Once Upon a Pizza
featuring Francesca™

33-Off to Winter Camp!
featuring Sandy™

Read more about **Our Generation®** books and dolls online:
ourgeneration.com

CONTENTS

EXTRA! EXTRA! READ ALL ABOUT IT!

*Big words, wacky words, powerful words, funny words…
what do they all mean? They are marked with this symbol *.
Look them up in the Glossary at the end of this book.*

Chapter One

THE FOUR WINDS

I sat up straight with my sheet music on my music stand. I held my recorder* up to my lips, and my fingers were ready. I should have been watching Ms. Flutter, who is our recorder teacher and our conductor*. But I sneaked a peek at the audience. All the kids in my whole school were out there, waiting for us to play. We were the last group to compete in the school talent competition.

We probably didn't have a chance against the fantastic dance routine just performed by a group of sixth graders. And the kindergarten choir was super cute. It's hard to beat out cuteness. But you never know!

"Sandy!" whispered Juanita, who sat beside me. "Get ready!"

Quickly, I looked at Ms. Flutter, who had been waiting to make sure all our eyes were on her. She tapped her baton* on her music stand, and then held up her hands. We were about to begin.

Normally, I'd be too nervous to join any kind of group all by myself. Plus, only two of us are in fourth grade—me and Rafael. I think Rafael is new to our school this year, but he isn't in my regular class during the day, so I'm not sure. And we don't sit beside each other in practice, so we've never talked.

The other five members of our group are in fifth and sixth grade. It's a small group, at least. I love music, and I was excited when Ms. Flutter said I could play the alto recorder, which is what I wanted. So, that's why I joined the recorder group in September. And it's been going alright. I enjoy the practices, and I don't feel as nervous as I once did.

There are four kinds of recorders in our group: soprano, alto, tenor, and bass. You play a recorder by blowing into it, which makes it a wind instrument. That's how we got our name, the "Four Winds."

Ms. Flutter waved her baton to count us in*—one, two, three, four…

And we began playing our piece. I was nervous at first, being in front of the whole school, but I know this piece so well. I had practiced it over and over at home. And soon I got caught up in the music and I even forgot we were onstage. I just

wanted to do my best.

And I did! We *all* did! We finished up without any of us making any major mistakes. Ms. Flutter looked pleased.

We filed off the stage and sat together with the other students who had competed.

Soon our principal, Mr. Corbett, stood onstage and asked for everyone's attention. He announced the third-place winner, then the second-place winner, and then the first-place winner: "The Four Winds!"

We won! We won! I was so excited.

But then—oh no. The prize.

"The Four Winds have won one week away at a winter camp for artistic kids up in the mountains," Mr. Corbett said from the stage. "There will be students from several schools, including other instrumentalists*, singers, actors, dancers, and so on.

"The Four Winds will get a chance to practice a new piece with a professional musician each day. You'll perform for the entire camp at the end of the week. And every day, you'll have a chance to enjoy different winter activities.

"Congratulations to the Four Winds!"

My heart sank.

Chapter Two

THE PRIZE

It's been almost a week since the concert. Of course, I had told Mom and Dad that my recorder group won the school talent competition. They were both excited for me, but…I still hadn't given them the permission form for camp. To be completely honest, I hadn't told them about the prize.

I don't want to go to winter camp!

I've gone on sleepovers at my best friend, Bianca's, house. She lives down the street from me and I've known her forever. Bianca goes to a different school than I do, and she has tons of friends there. Bianca is an extrovert*. She says I'm an introvert*. I'm not sure exactly what that means. But what I do know is that I like having one really good friend, and I'm also happy spending time on my own.

So, why should I go away to camp with my recorder group? I like my home. I like being on my own. I've never been away from home for a whole week, and I'm worried about being homesick.

And to top it off*, I don't like winter—at all. Especially being outside in the snow!

Here in Sunshine Valley, where we live, it hardly ever snows. But in the mountains up north, snow is pretty much guaranteed.

I still hadn't told anyone—not my music teacher or my music group, not my parents—that I don't want to go. But I told Bianca.

"Sandy, are you kidding?" Bianca said.

My best friend and I almost always spend Saturday together. We'd been up in my bedroom all morning, working on our paper doll collection.

Yes, we're probably the only kids in the whole world who still make paper dolls, but we don't care. We started a few years ago, and it's become one of our favorite things to do. We make figures in all shapes and sizes, and we love creating new clothing designs for them all.

So, we were hard at work with paper, cardboard, pencils, scissors, and colored markers when I made my confession* to Bianca.

"Sandy," Bianca said again. She put her hands on

her hips and looked at me sternly*. "You have to tell your parents about the prize. And you have to go to winter camp!

"There are only seven kids in your recorder group, and you're one of them. Your group needs you so you can all learn that new piece at camp and perform it together. You can't let them down."

Then she smiled. "Besides, winter camp could be awesome! Dress warmly and do lots of stuff outdoors, and you might just end up liking the cold and snow."

I made a face.

"I love being your best friend, but you need some friends at school, too," she went on. "Join in and talk to people. You have to be a friend to make a friend. I know you can do it if you try."

I made another face. Then I said, "OK, OK, I'll tell my parents. I'll show them the permission form and ask them to sign it. Are you done?"

Bianca grinned. "For now!"

"Good, 'cause I'm hungry!" I laughed, and we headed to the kitchen to make some sandwiches for lunch.

That evening, after dinner, I dug around in my backpack for the permission form. *Maybe it won't be there*, I hoped. But no, I found it.

I slogged* my way into the living room and handed it to Mom.

"What's this?" she asked, looking up from her laptop computer. She smoothed out the crumpled paper. As she read, her face lit up. "Oh, Sandy!"

"What's up?" Dad asked, lowering his magazine.

Mom quickly read the form aloud, including the descriptions of the prize, the winter camp, the basic schedule of the practices, and some of the activities.

"Snowshoeing, cross-country skiing, skating, snow tubing—! That sounds wonderful!" Mom said.

"I'd miss a week of school though," I said quickly. "I'm not sure that's such a good idea."

Dad raised his eyebrows.

"And I've never been away from home without you guys. You might really miss me," I warned them.

Mom's mouth twitched.

"I'll totally understand if you say no," I said.

Mom closed her laptop and Dad put down his

magazine.

"Sandy," Mom said, "thank you for worrying about us and for being so conscientious* about missing school. But this sounds like an amazing opportunity."

She got the dreamy look on her face that she always gets when she remembers her childhood. And sure enough—

"When I was girl, and we lived in upstate New York, my friends and I went sledding every weekend in the winter," Mom said. "And we'd go skating on the outdoor rink up the street."

"When I grew up in Minnesota, I was on my high school's cross-country ski team," said Dad. He had the same dreamy look on his face. "It was so much fun, Sandy! Bundling up and heading out across the fresh snow on our skis. We'd work up a real sweat, even though the air was cold."

I sighed. Mom and Dad went on and on about all the winter fun they had when they were kids, and I knew. I could see the writing on the wall*.

I would be going to winter camp, whether I wanted to or not.

Chapter Three

WHY DID I COME?

"You packed your snow pants and your two pairs of long underwear, right? And your pajamas, slippers, and hot water bottle?" Mom asked for the thousandth time.

"Yes, Mom," I told her.

She handed my duffel bag to the bus driver, and he loaded it into the baggage hold. It was getting crowded under there. We had been a bit late leaving home. Maybe, just maybe, I was hoping that, if I was a slowpoke*, I might miss the bus—and camp—altogether.

But no, although I was among the last to arrive, it looked like we'd made it on time. Our group was going in a large charter bus to the camp with groups from three other schools.

"Are all the other Four Winds players already on the bus?" Mom asked, looking around. "Oh, there's Ms. Flutter!"

Ms. Flutter waved in our direction from the bus steps. Just behind her was Ms. Trill, a student teacher. She was also coming to help supervise us at camp.

"Oh, good, you're here, Sandy!" Ms. Flutter called out. "Come along!"

Mom gave me a quick hug and kiss, and I hurried onto the bus with the bus driver right behind me.

The bus was almost full. As I headed down the aisle, I saw that the six other Four Winds had already paired up and were all sitting together at the front. There were some empty seats near the back.

I dropped down into one of the back seats and scooted over to the window. As the bus started up, Rafael got up from his seat and hurried down the aisle.

"Is it OK if I sit here?" he asked.

"Sure," I said. I guess he was trying to be nice.

As the bus pulled away from the parking lot, I waved goodbye to Mom. I had a lump in my throat*.

But then, Rafael began talking to me. He told me he had moved here with his family from Florida this past autumn and started at our school in October. He said it was hard missing the first month. He had to catch up on lots of schoolwork and it was awkward making new friends.

"But it's much better now," he said with a grin. "And I have two brothers and three sisters, and two of my grandparents live next door to us, and my aunt and uncle and two cousins live down the street, so it's not like I can ever really get lonely!"

I smiled.

Rafael told me about each of his brothers and sisters, and his cousins too. I just nodded and smiled. I slowly began to feel better.

"So, down in Florida, we never had snow. And I know there isn't much in the valley here. But these mountains—" Rafael frowned a bit. "Sandy, can you tell me...I'm a bit worried—"

He paused. "I've heard of the famous yeti. He's like an abominable snowman, right? A big, hairy, scary creature that only lives in the snow?" He looked at me intently.

The famous yeti? "Yeah, I guess so! I don't really know much about yetis," I said.

"Are there yetis in the mountains, Sandy? Do you

think they might be near where the winter camp is?" Rafael asked. "I'm not exactly sure I want to run into one."

Was he kidding? No, Rafael actually looked concerned!

"They probably don't even exist, but if they do, I'm pretty sure they only live in the Himalaya mountains. That's across the ocean on another continent," I said. "So you definitely don't need to worry."

"Oh, I don't know about that," Rafael said. "When I found out we were going on this trip, I did some research. It's possible some of the yetis crossed over from Asia to the North American continent hundreds of years ago. You know, when the Bering Strait land bridge* existed. If they did—if even *one* did—he or she could have ended up here."

"Well—" I said.

"It's possible, right?" Rafael insisted.

I was pretty sure it was impossible. But I also liked that Rafael was making it easy for me to talk with him. I wanted to be friendly. "Well, I don't know—"

"It's OK. We can ask someone at the camp when

we get there," he said. "They'll know for sure."

"Yeah, maybe," I said. "Or maybe we can just find a computer there and do more research on our own."

No way was I going to ask anyone at the winter camp about whether there were snow monsters around! I liked Rafael, but I didn't want everyone laughing at us. That would not be a great way to begin the week.

We stopped along the way for dinner, so it was evening when we arrived. We all climbed down from the bus and—*brrr*! There was a foot of snow on the ground. It was cold. Even the stars looked cold in the sky. I was already regretting coming.

As our bags were being unloaded, a woman came over and asked all of us in the Four Winds to gather around.

"Welcome, everyone! My name's Moira. I'm a group leader here at Camp Snow-Fun—where we work hard to show you that winter camp is no fun without snow fun!"

I laughed when she said the name of the camp.

"The main lodge* is right here," she said, pointing to a large log building with a big, wide covered porch. "Now, can you all grab your bags? I'm going to take you to your cabins and let you get settled, and then we'll meet back at the lodge."

The seven of us, and Ms. Flutter and Ms. Trill, gathered our backpacks and bags. Then we tromped after Moira along the snowy trail toward a row of little log cabins.

As we walked, I could hear Paula, one of the sixth graders in our group, talking to the other sixth graders, Gina and Juanita. "I've gone to summer and winter camp with my family so many times," she was saying. "I'm pretty much an expert at most winter sports—you know, like skating, snowshoeing—and I know lots of winter camping skills too." She sounded almost bored.

"Here we are," said Moira. "Four Winds, this is your cabin for the week."

The log cabin was simple but cute inside. It had a small main room with a little fireplace. It had a tiny kitchen, several doors leading off the main room, and a ladder that led up to a loft.

"The cabin is heated, so don't worry—you'll all be toasty warm!" Moira explained. It was like she'd read my mind.

"There are three bedrooms down here, and the loft up there," she went on. "Plenty of beds and bunk beds for all of you. Now, I'm off. I'll see you at the lodge in half an hour!"

Right away, I got butterflies in my stomach. *Bunk beds? I've never slept in a bunk bed. And Moira said it would be warm, but what if the heat goes out?* I thought.

Plus, I know how bad it feels to be picked last for a sports team in gym class. Or when we need to have a partner for class projects. *What if none of the other girls choose me as a roommate?*

Oh, why did I come?

Chapter Four

YETIS ARE DEFINITELY NOT REAL

"I want to be with Juanita and Gina, and—" Paula was saying in a loud voice. She turned to look at the two girls beside her.

My heart sank. It was happening. I thought of Bianca. Why had I let her talk me into coming?

But Ms. Flutter clapped her hands.

"Here are your room assignments," she said, with a smile. "Ms. Trill and I will be in this room," she said, pointing to the middle bedroom. "Rafael and Dan, you'll be in the one on the left. Juanita and Gina will share the other one. Paula, Yasemin, and Sandy will be up in the loft."

I glanced at Paula. She frowned and looked like she was going to argue with Ms. Flutter, but Juanita and Gina didn't seem upset. Dan, one of the fifth graders, immediately charged toward his room. Then everyone else was grabbing their bags and heading for their rooms. So, Paula grabbed hers and hurried to the ladder.

By the time I climbed up the ladder to the loft, Paula's bag was open on a single bed. She had almost finished unpacking. On the other side of the loft stood bunk beds.

Yasemin, the other fifth grader, came up behind me, grinned, and rolled her eyes. I smiled back.

"Top or bottom bunk?" she asked me. "Either is fine with me."

"Top, I guess," I said.

Even before Yasemin and I started to unpack, Paula was long gone. And I was regretting choosing the top bunk. What had I been thinking? What if I fell out?

But I didn't want to say anything to Yasemin. She was being really nice, chattering away. I didn't want to seem unfriendly by asking her to switch.

We finished unpacking and joined the rest of our group. We scrambled to put our jackets and boots back on and then headed up to the lodge with our teachers.

It was warm and cozy inside the large open space. I loved the fire roaring in the big stone fireplace. Lots of kids were already hanging out, and oh! There was a hot chocolate stand!

"Welcome, welcome! I'm Ms. Romero, the Camp Director!" called a friendly woman, standing on the hearth of the fireplace. She spread her arms wide as if she wanted to hug us all. "I'm glad you're all here! And I repeat, you're welcome to help yourself to our hot chocolate and snack dispenser anytime—including right now!"

"I want one! Sandy, stay here and I'll get you one too," Yasemin said to me, and then headed off.

Ms. Romero went on to describe the camp schedule. "You'll have your artistic practice first thing each morning. In the afternoons, we've planned fun activities, such as snowshoeing, skiing, a snowman competition, and so on. After dinner, we have evening activities for you to enjoy, including campfires, stargazing, and storytelling."

As she continued, Rafael came to stand next to me.

I grinned, and whispered, "You've got whipped cream on your nose!"

He laughed as he wiped it off. "Thanks!"

"Every group will spend a night camping out in our special tents," Ms. Romero said. "And on Saturday, our final afternoon, there will be a show. You'll all share with the other groups what you've been working on all week!"

Ms. Romero introduced the three special teachers who were here for the week: one for music, one for dance, and one for drama. She introduced the Head Outdoor Leader, Frank, and his staff of group leaders, including Moira, plus the chef, the kitchen staff, and the maintenance crew.

"Any questions?" she asked.

To my surprise, Rafael raised his hand.

"I have one. Ms. Romero, is there a yeti in your forest?" he asked.

I couldn't believe it! Lots of the other kids laughed, and I was super embarrassed!

The Director smiled, but in a nice way. "Well, maybe you'll hear some stories about yetis around the campfire one evening," she said.

Next, Ms. Romero explained that there were talent competition winners from eight schools here. She called out the name of each school's group, and when she did, the kids and their teachers stood up. She called out our name last—"The Four Winds!"

I stood up with my group in front of the other groups, and it felt good. For the first time, I began to feel like a real part of the Four Winds.

But the good feeling didn't last long. Back at the cabin, after I'd climbed up into my bunk, I began worrying again.

Yasemin was being nice to me, and Rafael too, but what if they ended up ignoring me tomorrow and I started to feel lonely? What if I got homesick? What if I fell off the top bunk during the night?

Plus, even though yetis are definitely not real, I started worrying about them. What if one was prowling around outside, or broke into our cabin?

I must have fallen asleep eventually, but during the night, half-awake, I woke up because someone was sniffling. Was it Yasemin? Maybe. Probably. Was she homesick?

I was trying to figure out what to do when the sound stopped. I snuggled into my warm blankets with my hot water bottle and fell back to sleep right away.

Chapter Five

STRANGE TRACKS

The next morning, we all had a yummy pancake breakfast up at the lodge, but I couldn't forget the sniffling I'd heard during the night. When we went back to our cabin to get our recorders, I got up my courage. I asked Yasemin if I could walk over to our first recorder practice session with her.

But Yasemin seemed so cheerful this morning. Maybe I'd make her sad again if I mentioned hearing her cry. Maybe I'd embarrass her. I wasn't sure what to say!

I decided to confide* some of my own worries, just to make her feel better.

"I was a bit homesick last night," I told her. "This is my first time away from home on my own. How about you? Have you been away from home much?"

"I've stayed at my friends' houses overnight a few times," she said. "It's fun. But, Sandy, I'm sorry you're feeling homesick."

So, she definitely didn't want to confide in me about her troubles, but I felt happy that I'd tried to make her feel better.

Our music practice was a bit shaky. Our camp music teacher, Mr. Dormer, started us on a new piece. Everyone made lots of mistakes and we were grumpy with one another.

"We have to perform in front of everyone on the last day," Paula complained afterwards, as we put away our recorders in the music room, "and we're going to sound terrible if we don't improve!"

"We have all week to learn the piece," Dan said. "No worries. We'll do fine."

But Paula shook her head. "We better!" she said.

We all headed over to the lodge. Yasemin and I got into the lunch line right behind Paula and Juanita. Rafael joined us.

"Did you notice, Sandy?" he said quickly. "Yesterday, I asked Ms. Romero about yetis, and she did *not* say there aren't any yetis around here!"

Before I could respond, Dan called out to Rafael,

and Rafael hurried over to join him.

Yasemin giggled. "What's all this about yetis?" she asked.

"Rafael moved here from Florida last fall, " I said. I told her about the conversation he and I had about yetis. "He's silly to worry about yetis. I told him they don't exist, but—" I grinned.

She giggled again.

But then Paula turned around. *Ack!* She'd heard us!

"Are you sure yetis don't exist, Sandy? Are you sure there aren't any in these woods?" she said, making big eyes at me. "Wouldn't it be scary if we saw one?"

Was she joking or not? I couldn't tell. I glanced at Yasemin, and it looked like she couldn't tell either. Then it was our turn to grab trays and choose our food. So, Paula took her tray and hurried after Juanita, and we started talking about something else.

"You have your choice of three outdoor activities today," said Frank, the Outdoor Leader. "Snowshoeing, cross-country skiing, or skating."

I really wished I could just snuggle up in the warm lodge and not go outside in the cold. But then I remembered what Bianca told me—"Just try it! You might like it!"

So, I tried to think positively. I put up my hand for cross-country skiing. Rafael, Yasemin, and Paula also put up their hands, and so did some kids from other groups.

"I've never tried this before," Rafael said to me, as we headed toward the cross-country ski shed. "Have you?"

"Never," I replied. Just then, I noticed Paula step away, hurrying to a smaller shed that was off to the side. She peeked in the door, and then slipped inside.

I joined the short line-up. Frank was handing out skis and poles, helping everyone choose ones that were the right length.

Then he called out, "That's just the storage shed, Paula."

I looked over. Now Paula was coming around the side of the small shed, grinning.

"The cross-country ski and snowshoe shed is over here," Frank said.

Paula gave a little wave and headed toward us.

STORAGE
CAT'S EYE TRAIL

What was she doing? I wondered.

"OK, gang," Frank continued. "Everyone has skis and poles? I'll show the first-timers how to put your skis on and give you a quick lesson. The others can head off on the Crooked Tree Trail, one of our longer trails, with my assistant, Natalie."

The experienced skiers, including Paula, headed off. Frank was patient with the rest of us who had never skied before. He showed us how to swing our arms and stride along the snow. It went pretty well, and before I knew it, I was getting the hang of it!

He invited us to follow him on the Cat's Eye Trail, a short trail that loops around through the woods and back, and off we went. I fell a few times, but it was nice being out in the woods. And I never got cold. The exercise kept me warm.

We completed the loop and headed back. I was at the end of the line of skiers, behind Rafael. I stopped for a moment to catch my breath when—what were those? I peered into the snow. Near the trail were some strange tracks.

I stepped off the trail to take a closer look. The

tracks were too big to be dog paw prints. Or wolf prints even. They were huge, and each one had five huge claws. I shuddered.

Were they…? They couldn't be.

Ahead of me, Rafael stopped and looked back. "Are you OK?" he called. "Want me to come and give you a hand?"

"I'm fine!" I replied. "I'll be right there!"

I quickly stepped back on the trail and hurried to catch up. I knew exactly what he'd think if he saw those tracks. He'd say they were yeti tracks because…well, they sort of looked like they might be!

Except it was impossible.

Chapter Six

MORE TRACKS

I slept like a log* that night. All the skiing, the falling, and getting back up again tired me out! I did wake up once and thought I heard sniffling. Was Yasemin still feeling homesick? But when we headed off to breakfast together in the morning, she was as cheerful as ever.

Our second recorder practice went a little better. We all still made lots of mistakes, but Mr. Dormer was encouraging. He had us break up to practice our parts separately. When we came back together as a group, the piece began to sound alright.

That afternoon, Frank announced that we had our choice of the same three outdoor activities—snowshoeing, cross-country skiing, or skating. Again, I couldn't help thinking how nice it would be to stay indoors by the fireplace, warm and cozy. But I shook it off.

When Yasemin decided to try snowshoeing, so did

Rafael. So did I. And, weirdly, Paula did, too.

We began in a group of about fourteen, but once again, by the time my boots were strapped in and I was ready to go, lots of kids, including Paula and Yasemin, had already disappeared down the trail. Rafael and I headed out at the end of the line.

We had lots of fun! Snowshoeing wasn't as easy as it looked, but it was easier than cross-country skiing. I wasn't cold at all. In fact, I'd worn too many layers.

"Hang on, Rafael!" I called out. "I have to stop and take off my jacket. I'm too hot!"

But I wish I hadn't. It gave Rafael a few minutes to rest and look around, and then suddenly—

"Sandy! Look! You'll never believe it!" He pointed down at the snow, off the trail. "Sandy, they have to be yeti tracks!"

Oh no! The tracks looked exactly like the ones I saw yesterday.

But I said, firmly, "No, Rafael. No, they're not." Although—was he right?

"What are they, then?" he asked. "They're huge!"

"Rafael, yetis don't exist, so these can't be yeti

tracks," I said. "Come on. Let's catch up to the others. We'll talk about it later."

Rafael and I got back and returned our snowshoes. As we entered the lodge, Yasemin and the other snowshoers were just gathering near the hot chocolate stand.

Yasemin waved to us. "Hey, you two! I'll get a drink for both of you!"

I saw her glance toward the fireplace. "Paula, we lost you on the trail! How did you get here so quickly?" Yasemin called.

Paula was already relaxing by the fire with a mug of hot chocolate.

"You all were just so slow," Paula said, looking a little uncomfortable. "I told you I've snowshoed before and I'm good at it, so I went on ahead."

I glanced at Yasemin, and we both rolled our eyes at the same time. But Rafael was tugging on my arm.

"Sandy, the yeti tracks," he said. "Who are we going to tell?"

"No one," I replied quickly. "Let's try to figure out

what we *really* saw. Stay here for a minute, OK?"

I walked over to Frank, who was standing near the reception desk, and asked if he had any information about paw prints I could look at.

"Sure," said Frank. He searched behind the counter, and then handed me a chart that said *Guide to Animal Tracks*. "Why? What did you see?"

I was too embarrassed to explain, especially because Paula was sitting so close by.

"Nothing, really. We're just interested in case we see any," I replied, as I hurried back to Rafael.

Rafael and I began studying the chart closely.

Yasemin came over with mugs of hot chocolate for us both and was instantly curious. Rafael, looking worried and excited, explained what had happened in a quiet voice.

"But none of these prints are as big as the ones we saw," he said.

"He's right," I agreed.

"Whoa," Yasemin breathed. "I wish I'd seen them too! So, you think it might be…"

"We don't know what it is yet," I told her quickly. "We need to do more investigating."

I wasn't sure what I meant by that, but it seemed to calm Rafael and Yasemin. Then we were all distracted by dinner and evening activities, and it was time for bed.

Ms. Flutter and Ms. Trill led all of us back to our cabin. The snow was just starting to fall in pretty little soft flakes. The porch light was on, and I knew it would be warm and snug inside.

Paula said goodnight to Juanita and Gina, and then was ready for bed first, as usual.

While Yasemin and I finished changing, Paula lay in bed. She was eating a pack of candies, even though we had all brushed our teeth, *and* we weren't supposed to bring our own treats to camp.

She kept looking up at us with this funny expression on her face, almost like she wanted one of us to say something about it. But there was no way I was going to complain to her!

I was about to climb up into my bunk, but then I thought about Yasemin crying in the night.

"Hey, Yasemin," I said to her quietly. "You can snuggle up on the top bunk with me if you want."

"Sure, that'd be fun! Are you still feeling homesick?"

she asked.

"No, I'm not!" I said, and I surprised myself. I was enjoying myself at camp. "I just thought you might be."

"Nope, I'm fine!" she said. "But it does sound like fun to have a sleepover with you," she giggled. "Thanks for the invite!" And she climbed up the ladder, bringing her blanket and pillow with her.

Of course, Paula said, "Don't you two dare keep me awake with your giggling!" which only made us giggle more.

But soon, we drifted off to sleep, side by side.

Chapter Seven

SEEING IS BELIEVING

Time seemed to be speeding up. Our morning recorder practice whizzed by. Mr. Dormer had some other fun pieces for us to try out, and then one of the student singing groups joined us and sang along to some of the new music.

After lunch, Rafael told us he'd never been snow tubing before and he really wanted to try it. I had gone snow tubing when I was a little kid visiting my grandparents in Minnesota, but I got snow in my face and up my nose and didn't like it!

Rafael asked Yasemin and me to go with him. He said *please* about a hundred times and put on the saddest face ever.

"Sure," Yasemin said, laughing.

And I finally gave in and said, "OK!"

Paula must have overheard us because she instantly

said that snow tubing was for little kids. She told us that she wanted to go skating because she had been taking skating lessons since she was a child.

"If you all want to skate, I'll even help you," she said. "I'm really good at it."

We just nodded and said thanks, but that we had decided to go snow tubing.

And for some reason, Paula actually decided to come with us.

Rafael fell out of the snow tube at first, but Paula was a really good sport, and she helped us take turns brushing him off and chasing after the tube.

Yasemin screeched as loudly as she could as she shot down the hill. "It's just like being at the amusement park," she cried happily.

And although I wrapped my scarf around my mouth and nose to protect my face from the snow, eventually, I was laughing too much to bother.

When she started getting tired, Paula even went up to the lodge and came back down with hot chocolate for the four of us. We sat together on a log bench and enjoyed listening to Paula tell us about the skating competitions

she'd been in and the medals she'd won.

After a little while, Yasemin, Rafael, and I decided to take one final run. But—it was strange—Paula looked at us funny. Like she didn't know what to do.

"I'm meeting up with Juanita and Gina now," she said suddenly and headed off. Would we have invited her to continue hanging out with us? Maybe. But before we could even think about it, she was gone.

The three of us headed toward the sports shed to return our snow tubes. But as we tromped up the hill, Rafael gasped.

"Look!" he said, standing stock-still*.

"Oh, wow," Yasemin breathed. "Rafael, you're right. They *are* yeti footprints!"

"Yasemin, no," I said, as I moved closer to look. "They just can't be. You know yetis are imaginary!"

"Well, I thought that. But seeing is believing, isn't it?" Yasemin asked. "Shouldn't we tell someone? What if it's—dangerous?"

Rafael and Yasemin looked at me, and I'm not sure why. Maybe because I sounded so sure of myself, even though I wasn't!

What they didn't know was the main reason I didn't want to mention the yeti tracks to anyone. I was more scared of being embarrassed in front of everyone at camp than I was scared of a yeti!

But, how could I say that to them? I was just beginning to feel like we were all becoming friends. Would they want a friend who was such a coward?

"Just…let's just think about it a little longer," I said, finally. "Maybe there's some way we can find out what other possibilities there could be. We…we don't want to scare the other kids without knowing for sure."

Yasemin and Rafael thought for a moment, and then they agreed. *Whew!*

There were only two more days left of camp. Maybe we wouldn't see any more footprints and we could all go home without announcing to the world that we thought there were yetis at camp!

Chapter Eight

WHAT'S UP, PAULA?

"OK, everyone. Let's try it one more time," Mr. Dormer said patiently.

Yasemin and I exchanged glances. Paula had made another bad mistake in our new piece. We'd all been improving, even her. But today, she didn't seem to be able to concentrate.

As we packed up our recorders for the day, Mr. Dormer said, "Remember, Four Winds, tomorrow is Friday. We have one more practice in the morning. Then on Saturday, you'll perform along with all the other groups in the big show."

"What's wrong with Paula?" Yasemin asked me as we walked to lunch together a few minutes later.

"I don't know," I said. I was just as puzzled as she was. Although now that I thought about it, I'd heard sniffling in the night again. Yasemin insisted *she* wasn't homesick or worried about anything else. Could it be Paula sniffling? But…why?

After lunch, Yasemin and I were back at the cabin, in the loft, bundling up in our outdoor clothes for our afternoon activity. But Paula just sat on the bed, munching on candies again.

"What's up, Paula?" Yasemin asked.

Paula pretended not to hear.

"Paula," Yasemin repeated. "Are you OK?"

"Yes, of course," she said.

"Why aren't you getting ready for the sleigh ride?" I asked. "It'll be so much fun!"

"I'm staying here this afternoon," she said in an abrupt voice. She didn't look at either of us.

What? There had to be something wrong.

Yasemin made a face at me and headed for the ladder. "Let's go, Sandy," she said.

"OK," I said, but I looked at Paula again. Should I say something more? Or maybe she just wanted to be left alone for a while. Maybe I'd embarrass her if I asked any more questions.

I stood there uncertainly.

"Sandy! Come on!" Yasemin called.

"I'll see you later at the campout," I said to Paula. She mumbled something, and I climbed down the ladder.

As I ran to catch up with Yasemin, I saw Ms. Flutter heading into our cabin. That was good. Paula wouldn't be left alone.

Rafael called out hello as Yasemin and I met up with our group in front of the lodge. All the other groups had gathered as well. A warmly dressed driver sat high on the front seat of a gleaming sleigh harnessed to two large brown horses. There were two empty rows of seats behind him.

"Students, please welcome Albert and his fine horses, Della and Clyde, to winter camp," Ms. Romero called. "Each group will get a turn to greet the two horses and go for a sleigh ride in the woods. The Twinkle Toes dance troupe* is first. The rest of you may wish to enjoy a snack or hot chocolate in the lodge while you wait."

"I'm going to wait out here," I told Yasemin and Rafael, as several of the groups headed into the lodge. "I'm too excited to go inside!"

The other Four Winds wanted to stay outside too. So, we all waited out in the snow, making snow angels and playing freeze tag together to pass the time. And when Albert returned with the horses and sleigh, it was our turn to go next.

The six of us, and Ms. Trill, took our time patting the horses and then got settled on the sleigh.

Albert cried, "Hep! Hep!" Off the horses went.

It was so beautiful. Della and Clyde pulled us down the snow-covered trail, deep into the woods. The bells on their harnesses jingled. We were all snuggled up under blankets. The sleigh runners* swished through the snow.

And even though I kept my eyes peeled*, there weren't any yeti tracks to be seen. *Phew!*

We had such an awesomely long ride. On the way back, Albert offered each of us a chance to sit beside him and drive. Dan and Gina said no, but everyone else said yes, including me. Yes, I actually held the reins and guided the two horses. I couldn't stop smiling. And I couldn't wait to tell Bianca!

Only one thing didn't feel right: Paula wasn't there.

She had missed out on the fun. But that was OK—it was the Four Winds' turn to camp overnight in tents tonight!

I shivered. From the cold, from excitement, from being a tiny bit afraid? Maybe all three, because yes, I did feel a little nervous about tonight.

It was one thing to go away from home for the first time and sleep in a cabin with other students from my school and my teachers. But to sleep out in small tents, in the woods, in the dark?

Chapter Nine

SPOOKY STORIES

"I'll tell the first campfire story," Frank said. "It's not at all scary. Well…maybe it's a bit scary."

I shivered again, but this time it was definitely from excitement.

I'd been so worried about being cold on this overnight, but each tent had a wooden floor, cots for our sleeping bags, and its own heater. We each had a flashlight, and each tent had two lanterns. I was sharing a tent with Yasemin. I felt safe and snug, and super happy!

Already, we had roasted hot dogs and veggie hot dogs over the fire.

Frank had brought three telescopes. The sky was full of stars! Frank let us peer at them through the telescopes. He told us their names and pointed out several constellations*.

All of us Four Winds were sitting around a bonfire

in the woods, roasting marshmallows on long sticks. Even Ms. Flutter and Ms. Trill were joining in. Our row of tents was behind us.

Frank began his story.

"My great-uncle Pete was worried. He was hearing strange sounds in his house, and he didn't know what was causing them. I offered to come and help. When I arrived it was late. He said thanks, but he was moving out until he knew the house was safe. I decided to stay over. I lay down on the couch in the living room and turned out the light.

"I was falling asleep when I heard a faint sound—*rap, rap, rap*.

"Where was it coming from? I got up to look.

"I listened at the bottom of the stairs. *Rap, rap, rap* came from the top of the stairs. So, I climbed up."

Yasemin, who sat on one side of me, snuggled closer.

"I heard it again—*rap, rap, rap*. It was coming from the attic. So, I climbed up the attic stairs."

Rafael, on my other side, also moved closer.

"I went into the attic," Frank continued, his voice quavering. "*Rap, rap, rap!* The sound came from the far

side of the attic.

"I walked toward it. I saw a big chest. It was shaking. *Rap, rap, rap!*

"I reached down. As I opened the chest—"

Yasemin and Rafael pressed even closer to me.

"RAP, RAP, RAP!

"I looked inside, and saw—" Frank paused dramatically.

I held my breath.

"A roll of *wrapping paper!*"

I burst out laughing. Yasemin and Rafael, and all the other Four Winds did too!

Then, Rafael said he had a story to share with our group. That didn't surprise me—I'd discovered that Rafael was friendly and outgoing. But the looks of surprise on the faces of the other kids told me I wasn't the only one who hadn't known Rafael very well before this week.

I just hoped it wasn't going to be a story that involved yetis!

"Wonderful," said Frank. "Please go ahead!" He threw another log on the bonfire, and the fire got brighter.

"This is a true story about a journey to a final

destination," Rafael began, making his voice sound spooky. "My grandmother told it to me, and I'm happy to share it with you. I just hope you can all sleep tonight after I'm finished."

Was he kidding? Probably, and yet—.

"One evening, my grandmother's mother got a message—to follow the long, dark road. What made her follow the instructions? To this day, no one knows."

He paused and looked at each of us, long and hard.

"She set off down the long, dark road, and at the end of the long, dark road was a long, dark path," he said. "At the end of the long, dark path was a lone, dark house."

He paused again.

"The lone, dark house had a single, dark door. Behind the single, dark door was a long, dark hall.

"At the end of the long, dark hall were some tall, dark stairs. And at the top of the tall, dark stairs was a long, dark balcony."

I swallowed. The wind rustled the branches on the trees. No one made a sound.

"At the end of the long, dark balcony was a big,

dark room," said Rafael. "In the big, dark room was a big, dark closet. In the big, dark closet was a big, dark door. And behind the big, dark door were some steep, dark stairs."

His voice got softer. "At the top of the steep, dark stairs was a dark, dusty attic. In the dark, dusty attic was a big, dark chest, and in the big, dark chest was a small, dark box."

He was almost whispering now. "And in the small, dark box was…"

Rafael paused dramatically. "…was…"

Juanita and Dan leaned forward, eyes wide. Gina was holding Ms. Flutter's hand.

Rafael yelled, "…was *a pink jelly bean!*"

We all burst out laughing.

Soon, Frank said it was time to get into our tents and go to sleep. It had been such a great day and such a great night. Nothing could spoil it!

Then—*Hoot! Hoot!*

An owl? Awesome! Everyone got quiet, listening.

Everyone except Rafael, who said, in a scared voice, loud enough for everyone to hear, "Is it a yeti?"

Chapter Ten

I'M NOT SCARED!

"A yeti?" echoed Dan.

Dan, Paula, Juanita, and Gina burst out laughing. Luckily, they seemed to think Rafael was continuing to joke.

"A yeti? Yeah, right," said Juanita. "Good one, Rafael!"

"You're funny!" Gina cried.

Ms. Flutter said, "OK, Four Winds. You heard Frank. It's time to say good night. Head for your tents please. I'll be around in a while to check that everyone is in their sleeping bags."

Frank began putting out the fire. Gina and Juanita headed for their tent.

Rafael and Dan, his tent partner, did too. But Paula hurried over to Rafael and held him back for a moment. I was still close enough to hear what she said.

"Listen, Rafael," Paula said to him in a low voice. "Yetis are definitely real. Yes, no one has ever taken a photo of a yeti, but that's because yetis are too fast to be caught on film. And are they here in these woods? Well, scientists have found long white hairs and skeletons near this camp. And *they can't identify them.*"

I had to speak up. "Rafael, that is not true. It isn't. Paula, don't scare Rafael!"

"I'm not scared," Rafael said. He strutted away toward his tent, but I could tell he was frightened.

I turned back to Paula, but she only shrugged and headed off toward the tent she was sharing with Juanita and Gina.

I don't know what woke me up that night, but something did. Something outside the tent. I was nervous, but I didn't want to get Yasemin scared too. So, I wiggled out of my sleeping bag, unzipped the tent flaps, and peeked out.

I couldn't see any stars out. Snowflakes swirled around. And there was Paula, coming out of her own tent.

Was she going to the outhouse*? Maybe. Or maybe not.

I kept watching.

Paula switched on her flashlight and she did head across the campsite to the outhouse. There was fresh snow, but you could see lots of footprints along the outhouse trail. There had been many visitors to the outhouse tonight.

But Paula didn't go inside! Instead, she shined her light under a nearby bush and bent down to pick something up. It looked like a snowshoe. She strapped it onto her right boot. Then she picked up another snowshoe and strapped it onto her left boot.

What was Paula up to?

I watched her walk awkwardly back along the well-trampled outhouse trail to the campsite area, but then—she headed straight for Rafael's tent! She marched across the snow, making fresh tracks right in front of it, and then did a complete circle around the tent. She ended up in front again, and then went back to where others had made the trail to the outhouse.

Paula slipped off the snowshoes. Wearing just her boots, she retraced her steps to the outhouse. She tucked the snowshoes back under the bush. Then she returned to

her own tent.

Two seconds later, I put on my jacket and boots, grabbed my flashlight, and went to examine the trail around Rafael's tent. Yeti prints!

What? How—? *Oh!*

The snowshoes had to be in the shape of yeti tracks! Paula had been using them to prank* Rafael all this time! *But why?*

Chapter Eleven

GOOD FRIENDS, LIKE US!

Yasemin and I were up early and I told her what I had seen during the night. Now we were ready, waiting, and watching.

Paula came out of her tent, yawning and stretching, casually glancing toward Rafael's tent.

Just then, Rafael stepped out of his tent. He waved at us, and then at Paula.

"Hey, what are those?" Paula cried. She went rushing over, pointing at the snow in front of Rafael's tent.

"What are what?" Rafael asked.

Paula stopped abruptly, speechless. Because there was nothing to see. Before going back to my tent last night, I had used a pine branch to sweep the yeti tracks away.

"Paula? What are what?" Rafael repeated. But Paula just shook her head, looking puzzled.

Dan came bursting out of the tent. "Raf, come on.

Let's go help Frank with breakfast," he cried, pulling on Rafael's arm. The two of them ran off.

"Paula," I said quickly, before she could walk away. "Do you believe in yetis? Really?"

Paula looked down at the snow. She folded her arms. "Yetis?"

"Yes, yetis," I said. "You told Rafael you do, but I'm pretty sure you know they aren't real. And I'm also sure you're good at making yeti tracks."

Paula's eyes opened wide.

"I saw what you did last night," I told her. "And I know it was you who made the yeti prints in the snow earlier this week too. I think you did it to scare Rafael. But I don't know why. Why would you want to scare him?"

Gina and Juanita came out of their tent. I thought they would call out to Paula, but they just walked on by.

"I'm sorry," Paula said. She bit her lip. "I'm really sorry I scared Rafael. I was planning to scare him and then save the day somehow. I hadn't quite figured that out yet."

"But why?" I asked. "Why would you do that?"

She looked down at the snow. "I was feeling left out. I thought that would make him like me, and if he did, you would both like me too."

"What? You feel left out?" said Yasemin. "But you have so many friends!"

"At school, maybe," Paula said. "But not here at camp. I'm not good friends with anyone in the recorder group. I try to tag along with Gina and Juanita, but they don't seem to care."

Paula's eyes filled with tears. "When I didn't come on the sleigh ride, I don't think they even noticed! You're the only one who did seem to care, Sandy."

She blushed. "I feel lonely here, and I don't like feeling that way. I haven't had to make new friends in a long time, and I'm not good at it. I realize how dumb that sounds," she sniffled.

"That does sound a little silly," Yasemin said.

Paula smiled back, and sniffled. And suddenly—*of course!* That sniffle—it was Paula crying in our room every night! I felt so bad.

"You went snow tubing with us," I reminded her, "and that was fun. Why didn't you just join in with us more often?"

"I'm not sure—" Paula answered. "I wasn't sure if

you really wanted me to. You didn't seem very friendly."

"Come on, girls!" Ms. Flutter called. "The pancakes are ready, and the maple syrup is hot!"

Yasemin headed toward the other Four Winds, who were standing around the cooking fire while Frank loaded up their plates, straight from the frying pan.

I decided to be brave once again. "Paula, honestly, I'm really terrible at making new friends. I'm amazed that Yasemin has somehow become my friend, and Rafael, too! I don't really know how it happened. And I certainly didn't think a sixth grader like you would ever want to be friends with me."

I smiled. "But if you want to hang out with Yasemin and me for what's left of camp—today and tomorrow morning—that would be great!"

Paula grinned as we gave each other a high five.

Paula, Yasemin, and I ate breakfast together and then the three of us walked to our last music practice. Paula played her part with a couple of tiny mistakes, but she didn't even grumble.

After lunch, the three of us made a snow fort, joined a big game of charades with kids in other school groups, and then had hot chocolate in the lodge.

And after dinner? The three of us made a huge yeti snowman outside our cabin. When they saw how much fun we were having, the other Four Winds joined in. Together, we made a whole yeti family!

Even better, Paula showed Rafael her blue plastic snowshoes. "I made all the yeti tracks," she said. "I'm sorry I tried to scare you."

Rafael just laughed and told her it was OK.

Paula smiled from ear to ear. She was so happy that she took a deep breath and told all the Four Winds about what she'd done. She suggested we could each try out her snowshoes.

When it was Gina's turn, I nudged Yasemin. Gina and Juanita were joking around with Paula, asking her to come with them while they made their yeti prints.

"They're going to end up being good friends, like us," Yasemin said to me.

"Just like us," I agreed.

Chapter Twelve

SMILE!

I sat up straight with my sheet music on my music stand. I held my recorder up to my lips, and my fingers were ready. We were about to begin playing in the camp show, and I should have been watching Mr. Dormer—but I sneaked a peek at Paula.

I hadn't heard any sniffling last night, which was wonderful. And this morning, Juanita and Gina asked Mr. Dormer if Paula could share their music stand with them, and he agreed. So, the three of them were crowded around it now, all ready to play. Paula's eyes were shining.

Mr. Dormer tapped on his music stand, lifted his hands, and waved his baton to count us in—one, two, three, four…

It was time to pack up and go! I could hardly

believe it. The week had flown by.

Yasemin, Rafael, Paula, and I hung around in front of the cabin after the other kids had taken their bags up to wait for the bus.

"I actually wish we could stay longer now," said Paula.

"Me too," I said, and I grinned. *Bianca will be so happy when I tell her I've done lots of fun things outside in the snow. And made some new friends,* I thought. I finally understood what Bianca has always told me: I have to be a friend to make a friend!

Ms. Trill and Ms. Flutter came out of the cabin after doing a final check of the place.

"Ready to head out?" Ms. Flutter asked. "The bus leaves soon."

Yasemin, Rafael, and Paula all nodded yes, but I said, "Oh, wait! Ms. Flutter, would you mind taking a photo of the four of us?"

"What a lovely idea," she said. "I'll make copies and send them to your parents."

We stood together—four Four Winds friends.

"Ready?" Ms. Flutter asked. "Smile!"

Glossary

*Many words have more than one meaning. Here are the definitions of words marked with this symbol * (an asterisk) as they are used in this story.*

baton: *a thin stick used by someone who directs a musical group as they play music*

Bering Strait land bridge: *a bridge of land that may have existed long ago and linked the continent of Asia with the continent of North America*

conductor: *a person who directs a musical group*

confession: *something that you tell someone else that you might be ashamed of or embarrassed about*

confide: *tell someone something secret that you don't want them to tell anyone else*

conscientious: *wanting to do what is right*

constellations: *groups of stars that form a certain shape and have been given a name*

count us in: *a way to let musicians know when it is the correct moment to begin playing by counting the musical beats*

extrovert: *an outgoing person who greatly enjoys being around other people*
instrumentalists: *musicians who play instruments*
introvert: *a person who may seem shy because they often enjoy being alone*
"kept my eyes peeled": *watched carefully*
lodge: *the main building of a camp*
"lump in my throat": *a tight feeling in the throat caused by a strong emotion, such as sadness*
outhouse: *an outdoor building with a toilet and no running water*
prank: *to play a trick on someone*
recorder: *a wooden or plastic instrument with holes that makes music when you blow air through it and cover different holes with your fingers*
runners: *curved pieces of metal attached under a sleigh that let it slide over snow*
"slept like a log": *slept well without moving*
slogged: *walked with slow, heavy steps*
slowpoke: *someone who moves slowly*
sternly: *in a serious way*

stock-still: *completely still*
"to top it off": *the last thing that happens to make an experience better, or worse, than all the things that happened before that*
troupe: *group of performers*
"writing on the wall": *a clue that something unpleasant is going to happen*

STRANGE TRACKS

When Sandy and her friends see tracks in the snow, they wonder: Could they be yeti tracks? To find out, they look at a *Guide to Animal Tracks*. Now it's your turn. Have a look at *these* animal tracks. See if you can match each one with its name on the list. Then check the answers on page 82.

Alligator
Elephant
Fox

Kangaroo
Lion
Lizard

Raccoon
Wolf
Yeti

Answers to STRANGE TRACKS:

1. Fox 2. Kangaroo 3. Alligator 4. Raccoon
5. Lizard 6. Yeti 7. Lion 8. Elephant 9. Wolf

this is **my** favorite winter fun story:

WE Charity

The Power of a Girl

For every *Our Generation®* product you buy, a portion of sales goes to WE Charity's Power of a Girl Initiative to help provide girls in developing countries an education—the most powerful tool in the world for escaping poverty.

Did you know that out of the millions of children who aren't in school, 70% of them are girls? In developing communities around the world, many girls can't go to school. Usually it's because there's no school available or because their responsibilities to family (farming, earning an income, walking hours each day for water) prevent it.

WE Charity has had incredible success in its first 20 years. Together, we've built more than 1,000 school rooms, empowering more than 200,000 children with an education. As WE Charity continues to deepen its programming, it's focusing on creating sustainable communities through its holistic development model built on the five Pillars of Impact: Education, Water, Health, Food and Opportunity.

The most incredible part about this model is that roughly a quarter of WE Charity's funding comes from kids just like you, who have lemonade stands, bake sales, penny drives, walkathons and more.

Just by buying an *Our Generation* product you have helped change the world, and you are powerful (beyond belief!) to help even more.

WE

Together we change the world.

WE Charity provided the factual information pertaining to their organization.
WE Charity is a 501c3 organization.

About the Author

Susan Hughes is an award-winning author of more than 30 children's books, including picture books, chapter books, young adult novels, nonfiction books for all ages, and even a graphic nonfiction book. Susan is also a freelance editor and writer. She helps coach and guide other writers in revising and polishing their own manuscripts.

About the Illustrator

Passionate about drawing from an early age, Géraldine Charette decided to pursue her studies in computer multimedia in order to further develop her style and technique. Her favorite themes to explore in her illustrations are fashion and urban life. In her free time, Géraldine loves to paint and travel. She is passionate about horses and loves spending time at the stable. It's where she feels most at peace and gives her time to think and fuel her creativity.

Off to Winter Camp! became the book that you are holding in your hands with the assistance of the talented people at Maison Battat Inc., including Joe Battat, Dany Battat, Sandy Jacinto, Loredana Ramacieri, Véronique Casavant, Cynthia Lopez, Laurie Gaudreau-Levesque, Alexandra Bonfà, Ananda Guarany, Arlee Stewart, Natalie Cohen, Joanne Burke Casey, Pamela Shrimpton, and Elizabeth Plummer.